SUPER SIMPLE
◀TRIANGLES▶

NANCY SMITH & LYNDA MILLIGAN

Book Production

Nancy Smith & Lynda Milligan

Sharon Holmes – Editor, Technical Illustrator

Lexie Foster – Cover & Graphic Design

Christine Scott – Graphic Design

Sandi Fruehling – Copy Reader

Brad Bartholomew – Photographer

Thanks

Sewers – Jane Dumler, Ann Petersen, Courtenay Hughes, Barbara
Karst, Katie Wells, Kelly Kiel, Sue Williams, Sandi Fruehling

Quilters – Ann Petersen, Jane Dumler, Laura Serota

Long-arm Quilters – Susan F. Geddes, Kay Morrison,
Sandi Fruehling, Debra Geissler

Doll on Front Cover – Jeannie Edwards of Art Out of da Box
& Art Dolls by Jean-Marie

POSSIBILITIES®

Fabric Designers for Avlyn, Inc. • Publishers of Possibilities® Books
Home of Great American Quilt Factory, Inc.
www.greatamericanquilt.com • www.possibilitiesquilt.com
1-800-474-2665

Super Simple Triangles
©2006 Nancy Smith & Lynda Milligan

SUPER SIMPLE SERIES *by Possibilities*®

We started our **Super Simple Series** with squares, moved on to strips, and continued with fat quarters.
These books have been so much fun that we decided to expand the series with the current book,
Super Simple Triangles. We truly hope you enjoy all four distinctively different Super Simple books.

Super Simple Squares
shows you the endless
combinations that can be
created by using fat quarters
or packets of precut 6½"
squares or strips. This book
contains 18 original quilt
designs with full directions
as well as a comprehensive
general directions section.
Yardage charts also include
amounts for purchasing
fabric off the bolt.

Super Simple Strips
features 18 fantastic quilts,
four with specially designed
applique. We offer ideas for
pieced backings, a great
way to utilize leftover
fabrics. Yardage charts
include amounts required
for purchasing fabric off
the bolt as well as precut
rolls or packets of 6½"
strips.

Super Simple Fat Quarter Quilts helps you make use of all those fat quarters you've
been collecting! This enticing book provides patterns for 12 amazing quilts made with
a variety of techniques. Explicit cutting diagrams show exactly how to cut the fat quarters
for each project. Layer-and-cut techniques make cutting easy and fun! Our paper triangle
grids for half-square triangle units provide you with the exact sizes needed.

So Many Methods

Tri an gle: a three-sided polygon.

In this book we work with right-angled, isosceles triangles, in other words, half-square triangles. We have used a number of different methods for making triangles, and we are sure you will enjoy trying them.

In the first method, fabric squares are cut in half to make triangles, then the triangles are sewn together to make squares which we call half-square triangle units. This method involves a little math— $7/8''$ is added to the size of the finished unit to get the size of the square, with the seam allowance added, that will be cut in half. The measurements of these squares usually involve $1/8''$ increments, so make sure your rotary ruler is marked in eighths. Half-square triangle units can be used in many ways— to make borders as in Zig and Zag, or to make the main part of a quilt as in Domino Effect.

Another technique uses foundation paper for making the triangle units. There are many triangle foundation products available, the two most common being Triangles on a Roll and Thangles™. Two pieces of fabric are placed right sides together, and the foundation product is placed on top. The quilter stitches on the dotted lines and cuts on the solid lines. Remove the paper, and you have perfectly pieced half-square triangle units. This technique can replace the first method described above. Be aware that more fabric may be needed.

For method three, fabric squares are folded and pressed to create triangles that are stitched into seams. These dimensional triangles add an element of fun to a quilt. In Happy Days, the pinwheels in the blocks and the triangles in the border are made with this method.

A fourth method also starts with a fabric square. A diagonal line is drawn from one corner to the opposite corner. This square is placed on a background fabric and the quilter stitches on the drawn line. One half of the square is then folded over the other half to create a triangle. The fabric behind the top triangle may be trimmed away, or if the unit is very small or the extra layer of fabric is not a problem, it can be left untrimmed. This method is used to make units for Park Avenue, Indigo and Eggplant, and Flower Power.

A final technique for making triangles involves cutting strips of varying widths, stitching them together into strip sets, and then cutting them into large triangles. This is a quick method for pieced triangles which creates very little waste. See the quilt Oriental Garden.

Value is Relative

After looking through this book, you will see that value is very important in many of these quilts. Before starting a quilt, arrange fabrics into lights, mediums, and darks. When choosing the fabrics for each patch, remember that value is relative. In a light and medium combination, the medium will act like a dark. If you have a hard time deciding, you might get a value tool from your favorite quilt shop. They are usually made from red or green plastic. When you look at the fabrics through a value tool, it is much easier to judge their relative value. The quilt Southern Comfort is an interesting study in values.

Create on Your Own

One of the great things about half-square triangle units is that you can make so many different quilt patterns from them. Units with one light side and one dark side can be rotated to create dozens of different blocks and whole-quilt designs. See page 45 for four more ideas for quilts using half-square triangle units. Quilts made from these diagrams will vary in size depending on the size of the triangle unit you choose to make and the widths of the borders you add.

Pressing

Follow our pressing directions for each step, and your quilt will piece together like magic!

The Good Earth
6″ Unit 61x79″

If using paper triangles for half-square triangle units, you may need more of some fabrics.

Yardage Choose fabric with 42″ usable width.

Units	2 yd dark
	½ yd each of 6 mediums
Border 1	⅓ yd
Border 2	½ yd
Border 3	1¼ yd
Binding	⅔ yd
Backing	5 yd
Batting	67x85″

Cutting Cut strips from selvage to selvage.
*Cut in half diagonally.

Units	*44 squares 6⅞″ dark
	*7-8 squares 6⅞″ of each medium
Border 1	6 strips 1¼″ wide
Border 2	6-7 strips 2″ wide
Border 3	7 strips 5″ wide
Binding	8 strips 2½″ wide

Directions Sew ¼″ seam allowances unless otherwise noted.

1. UNITS: Make 88 dark and medium half-square triangle units. Press seam allowances toward the dark.

  Make 88

2. ASSEMBLE: Arrange blocks in a setting of 8 across and 11 down with diagonal seams oriented as shown. Stitch blocks into rows. Press vertical seam allowances to right in odd rows and to left in even rows as shown by arrows. Stitch rows together. Press long horizontal seam allowances down or open.

3. BORDERS: For each border, stitch strips together end to end using straight, not diagonal, seams. Press. Cut 2 pieces to fit sides of quilt. Stitch to quilt. Press seam allowances toward outside edge of quilt. Repeat at top and bottom.

4. LAYER & QUILT: Piece backing vertically to same size as batting. Layer and quilt as desired. Trim backing and batting even with quilt top.

5. BIND: Stitch binding strips end to end. Press in half lengthwise, wrong sides together. Bind quilt using ⅜″ seam allowance.

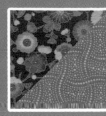

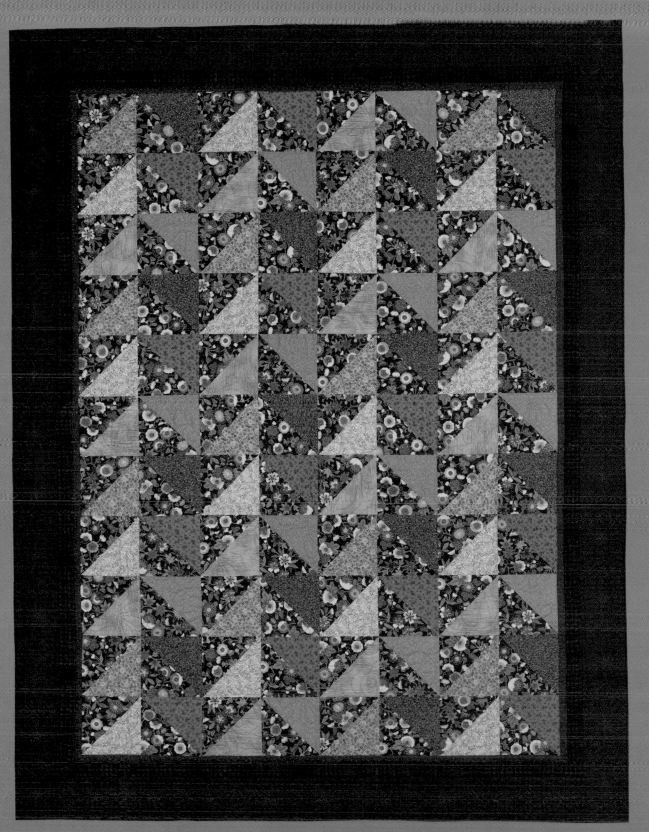

Kimono Blossoms
5″ Unit   72x92″

If using paper triangles for half-square triangle units, you may need more of some fabrics.

Yardage Choose fabric with 42″ usable width.

Units	⅝ yd each of 7 lights & 7 darks
Border 1	½ yd
Border 2	1½ yd
Binding	¾ yd
Backing	5⅞ yd
Batting	78x98″

Cutting Cut strips from selvage to selvage.
*Cut in half diagonally.

Units	*14 squares 5⅞″ of each light
	*14 squares 5⅞″ of each dark
Border 1	8 strips 1½″ wide
Border 2	8 strips 5½″ wide
Binding	9 strips 2½″ wide

Directions Sew ¼″ seam allowances unless otherwise noted.

1. UNITS: Make 192 light and dark half-square triangle units. Lightly finger press seam allowances so direction can be easily changed.

   Make 192

2. ASSEMBLE: Arrange units in a setting of 12 across by 16 down, orienting diagonal seams as shown. As you stitch units into rows, position all seam allowances, diagonal as well as vertical, to right in odd rows and to left in even rows. See arrows on diagram. Press. Stitch rows together. Press long horizontal seam allowances down or open.

3. BORDERS: For each border, stitch strips together end to end using straight, not diagonal, seams. Press. Cut 2 pieces to fit sides of quilt. Stitch to quilt. Press seam allowances toward outside edge of quilt. Repeat at top and bottom.

4. LAYER & QUILT: Piece backing vertically to same size as batting. Layer and quilt as desired. Trim backing and batting even with quilt top.

5. BIND: Stitch binding strips end to end. Press in half lengthwise, wrong sides together. Bind quilt using ⅜″ seam allowance.

KIMONO *Blossoms*

Domino Effect

4″ Unit 16″ Block 60x76″

If using paper triangles for half-square triangle units, you may need more of some fabrics.

Yardage Choose fabric with 42″ usable width.

Blocks	⅜ yd each of 8 lights & 8 darks
Border 1	⅝ yd
Border 2	1⅜ yd
Binding	⅔ yd
Backing	4⅞ yd
Batting	66x82″

Cutting Cut strips from selvage to selvage.
*Cut in half diagonally.

Blocks	*12 squares 4⅞″ of each fabric
Border 1	8 strips 2″ wide
Border 2	8 strips 5″ wide
Binding	8 strips 2½″ wide

Directions Sew ¼″ seam allowances unless otherwise noted.

1. BLOCKS: Make 192 light and dark half-square triangle units. Lightly finger press seam allowances so direction can be easily changed. Make 48 quarter-blocks, pressing as shown by arrows. Wait to press horizontal seam allowances until quarter-blocks are assembled into blocks. As you stitch quarter-blocks into blocks, alternate direction of unpressed seam allowances. Press blocks, leaving horizontal seam allowances unpressed until blocks are sewn into rows.

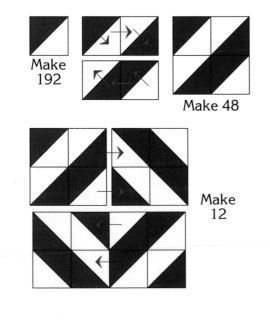

Make 192

Make 48

Make 12

2. ASSEMBLE: Arrange blocks in a setting of 3 across by 4 down, oriented as shown. Distribute fabrics evenly across quilt top. Stitch blocks into rows, alternating direction of unpressed horizontal seam allowances. Press remaining vertical seam allowances in odd rows to right and in even rows to left. Stitch rows together. Press long horizontal seam allowances down or open.

3. BORDERS: Stitch Border 1 strips end to end using straight, not diagonal, seams. Press. Repeat with Border 2 strips. Cut 2 pieces 66″ long from each. Stitch Border 1 and Border 2 pieces together. Press seam allowance toward Border 2. Make 2. Repeat with pieces 82″ long.

   Pin one of the short border units to top edge of quilt, right sides together, centered. Border should extend 9″ at each end. Stitch, leaving seam allowance free at each end. Press seam allowance toward outside edge of quilt. Repeat on bottom edge of quilt. Repeat on sides of quilt using longer border units.

   Press mitered corners on ironing board as shown. Stitch. Trim seam allowance to ¼″ and press open. Diagrams on page 42.

Continued on page 42

8

DOMINO *Effect*

Southern Comfort

3″ Unit 9″ Block 54 x 72″

If using paper triangles for half-square triangle units, you may need more of some fabrics.

Yardage Choose fabric with 42″ usable width.

Blocks   2⅝ yd light - background
         ⅙ yd each of 17 mediums
         ⅙ yd each of 8 darks
Binding ⅝ yd
Backing 3⅝ yd
Batting 60 x 78″

Cutting Cut strips from selvage to selvage.
*Cut in half diagonally.

Blocks   *216 squares 3⅞″ of light
         *10 squares 3⅞″ of each medium
         *6 squares 3⅞″ of each dark
Binding 7 strips 2¼″ wide

Directions Sew ¼″ seam allowances unless otherwise noted.

1. BLOCKS: Make 336 light/medium half-square triangle units and 96 light/dark units. Lightly finger press seam allowances so direction can be easily changed. As you stitch units into rows for each block, position seam allowances, diagonal as well as vertical, in direction shown by arrows. Press. Stitch rows together into blocks. Press horizontal seam allowances in direction of arrows. Make 48 blocks.

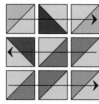

Make 336 with light/medium

Make 96 with light/dark

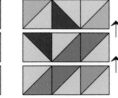 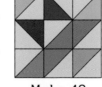

2 light/dark
7 light/medium

Make 48

2. ASSEMBLE: Arrange blocks in a setting of 6 by 8, oriented as shown. Stitch blocks into rows. Press seam allowances to right in odd rows and to left in even rows. Stitch rows together. Press long horizontal seam allowances down or open.

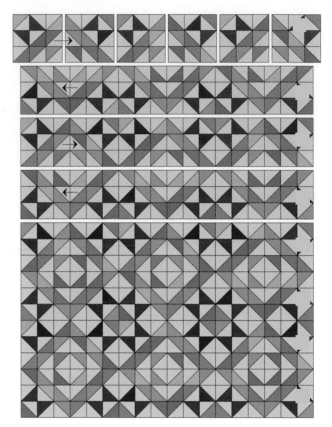

3. LAYER & QUILT: Piece backing horizontally to same size as batting. Layer and quilt as desired. Trim backing and batting even with quilt top.

4. BIND: Stitch binding strips end to end. Press in half lengthwise, wrong sides together. Bind quilt using ¼″ seam allowance.

SOUTHERN *Comfort*

Zig & Zag
4" Border Unit 48 x 64"

If using paper triangles for half-square triangle units, you may need more of some fabrics.

Yardage   Choose fabric with 42" usable width.

Center panel	1½ yd - if print is one-way directional, it must be on lengthwise grain
Border	⅝ yd yellow
	¾ yd green
	1 yd blue
Binding	⅝ yd green
Backing	3¼ yd
Batting	54 x 70"

Cutting   Cut strips from selvage to selvage.   *Cut in half diagonally.

Center panel	1 piece 32½ x 48½"
Border	*22 squares 4⅞" yellow
	*26 squares 4⅞" green
	*48 squares 4⅞" blue
Binding	6 strips 2¼" wide

Directions   Sew ¼" seam allowances unless otherwise noted.

1. BORDER: Make 52 green and blue half-square triangle units. Make 44 yellow and blue units. Lightly finger press seam allowances so direction can be easily changed. Stitch into double units, opposing seam allowances as shown by arrows. Press vertical seam allowances in direction of arrows. Reserve remaining units.

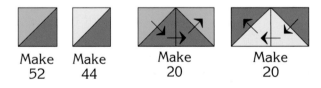

Make 52	Make 44	Make 20	Make 20

Using 5 blue and green double units for each border piece, make 4 as shown. Press remaining vertical seam allowances in direction of arrows. Repeat with blue and yellow double units.

Make 4

Make 4

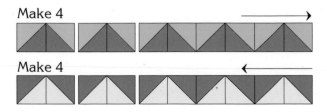

Stitch border pieces together as shown. Press seam allowances toward green.

Make 4

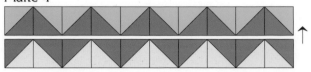

Stitch remaining half-square triangle units into double units for ends of borders. Press seam allowances in direction of arrows. Stitch to borders, oriented as shown. Press as shown.

Make 2 - Sides

Make 2 - Top & Bottom

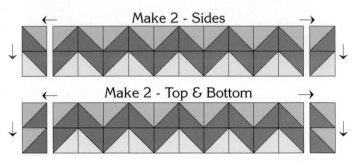

Stitch side borders to center panel. Press seam allowances toward center of quilt. Repeat with top and bottom borders.

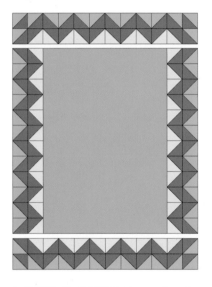

2. LAYER & QUILT: Piece backing horizontally to same size as batting. Layer and quilt as desired. Trim backing and batting even with quilt top.

3. BIND: Stitch binding strips end to end. Press in half lengthwise, wrong sides together. Bind quilt using ¼" seam allowance.

Irish Summer

8½″ Block   51x68″

Yardage
Choose fabric with 42″ usable width.

Blocks	center squares	1⅓ yd large floral
		more needed if fussy-cutting motifs
	corners	¼ yd each of 10 or more greens
Border		1 yd green
Trim		6 yd white jumbo ric-rac
Binding		⅝ yd green
Backing		3½ yd
Batting		57x74″

Cutting
Cut strips from selvage to selvage.
*Cut in half diagonally.

Blocks	center squares	35 squares 6½″
	corners	*7 squares 5⅛″ of each fabric
Border		6 strips 5″ wide
Binding		7 strips 2½″ wide

Directions
Sew ¼″ seam allowances unless otherwise noted.

1. BLOCKS: Make 35 blocks as shown using green fabrics randomly. Press seam allowances toward center of 18 blocks. Press seam allowances toward outside of 17 blocks.

   For each block:

   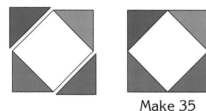

   Make 35

2. ASSEMBLE: Arrange blocks in a setting of 5 across and 7 down, alternating center-pressed blocks with outside-pressed blocks (top left block must be one with seam allowances pressed toward center of block). Stitch blocks together in horizontal rows. Press seam allowances between blocks open. Stitch rows together. Press seam allowances between rows open.

3. BORDER: Stitch strips together end to end using straight, not diagonal, seams. Press. Cut 2 pieces to fit sides of quilt. Baste ric-rac to border pieces, centered on seam line. Stitch to quilt. Press seam allowances to center of quilt. Repeat at top and bottom, tucking in ends of ric-rac at each end to finish at corner of quilt center.

4. LAYER & QUILT: Piece backing horizontally to same size as batting. Layer and quilt as desired. Trim backing and batting even with quilt top.

5. BIND: Stitch binding strips end to end. Press in half lengthwise, wrong sides together. Bind quilt using ⅜″ seam allowance.

IRISH Summer

Just Triangles

2″ Unit 4″ Unit 37x45″

If using paper triangles for half-square triangle units, you may need more of some fabrics.

Choosing variegated fabrics increases number of available colors in same yardage.

Yardage Choose fabric with 42″ usable width.

Blocks	1 yd white
	¼ yd each of 12 or more brights
Border 1	¼ yd pink-orange
Border 2	⅝ yd black
Binding	½ yd black
Backing	1½ yd
Batting	41x49″

Cutting Cut strips from selvage to selvage.
*Cut in half diagonally.

Blocks	4 squares 4½″ - white
	*10 squares 4⅞″ - white
	*60 squares 2⅞″ - white
	*30 squares 4⅞″ - brights
	*20 squares 2⅞″ - brights
Border 1	4 strips 1⅛″ wide
Border 2	4 strips 4½″ wide
Binding	5 strips 2½″ wide

Directions Sew ¼″ seam allowances unless otherwise noted.

1. UNITS: Make 19 half-square triangle units with triangles cut from 4⅞″ squares. Press seam allowances in direction of arrows.

Make
19

Make 40 half-square triangle units with triangles cut from 2⅞″ squares. Press seam allowances in direction of arrows. Make 40 double-triangle units by adding triangles cut from 2⅞″ and 4⅞″ squares. Press seam allowances in direction of arrows.

Make
40

Make 40

2. ASSEMBLE: Placing colors as desired, arrange units using black and white diagram as a guide.

Continued on page 36

Crooked Path
3″ Unit 54x69″

If using paper triangles for half-square triangle units, you may need more of some fabrics.

Yardage Choose fabric with 42″ usable width.

Units	⅙ yd each of 15 darks
	⅓ yd each of 15 lights
Border 1	⅓ yd
Border 2	⅞ yd
Binding	⅝ yd
Backing	3⅝ yd
Batting	60x75″

Cutting Cut strips from selvage to selvage.
*Cut in half diagonally.

Units	*7 squares 3⅞″ of each dark
	*13 squares 3⅞″ of each light
Border 1	6 strips 1¼″ wide
Border 2	6 strips 4½″ wide
Binding	7 strips 2½″ wide

Directions Sew ¼″ seam allowances unless otherwise noted.

1. UNITS: Make units. Lightly finger press seam allowances so direction can be easily changed.

 Make 210 with light/dark    Make 90 with light/light

Lay out first 3 rows, for Row Set 1, orienting diagonal seams as shown. See page 43 for diagram of all row sets.

Row Set 1

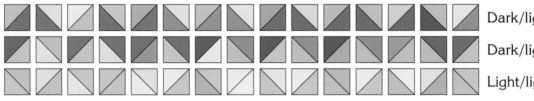

Dark/light units

Dark/light units

Light/light units

As you stitch units into rows, position seam allowances, diagonal as well as vertical, in direction of arrows as shown below. Press. Complete Row Set 1 by stitching rows together. Press seam allowances between rows down or open. Make Row Set 3 and Row Set 5 the same way.

Row Sets 1, 3, 5

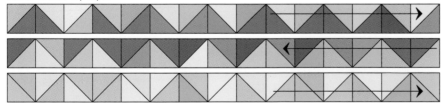

Continued on page 43

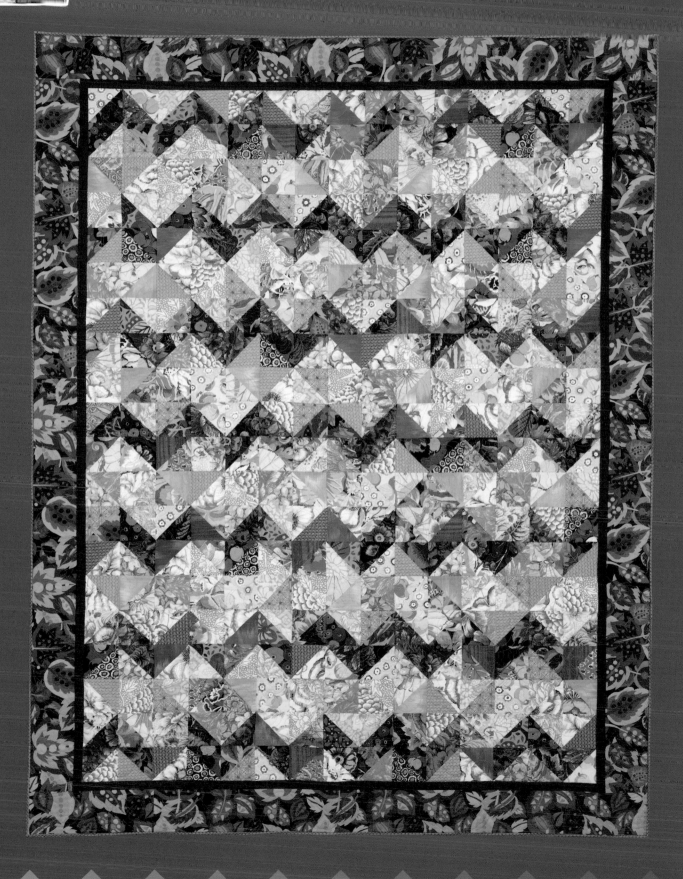

Fresh Breeze

2¼" Unit 3" Unit 9" Block 62x74"

If using paper triangles for half-square triangle units, you may need more of some fabrics.

Yardage Choose fabric with 42″ usable width.

Blocks	⅓ yd each of 12 or more blues
Setting fabric	1⅞ yd white
Border	1½ yd blue
Binding	⅔ yd blue
Backing	4⅛ yd
Batting	68x80″

Cutting Cut strips from selvage to selvage.
*Cut in half diagonally.
**Cut in quarters diagonally.

Blocks	*3⅞" squares as needed for half-square triangle units for Blocks A-E
	3½" squares as needed for plain squares for Blocks A-E
	*3⅛" squares as needed for half-square triangle units for Block F
Setting pieces	12 squares 9½"
	**4 squares 14" - sides
	*2 squares 7¼" - corners
Border	7 strips 6" wide
Binding	7-8 strips 2½" wide

Directions Sew ¼″ seam allowances unless otherwise noted.

1. BLOCKS: Make 20 blocks using fabrics as desired. Press seam allowances in direction of arrows.

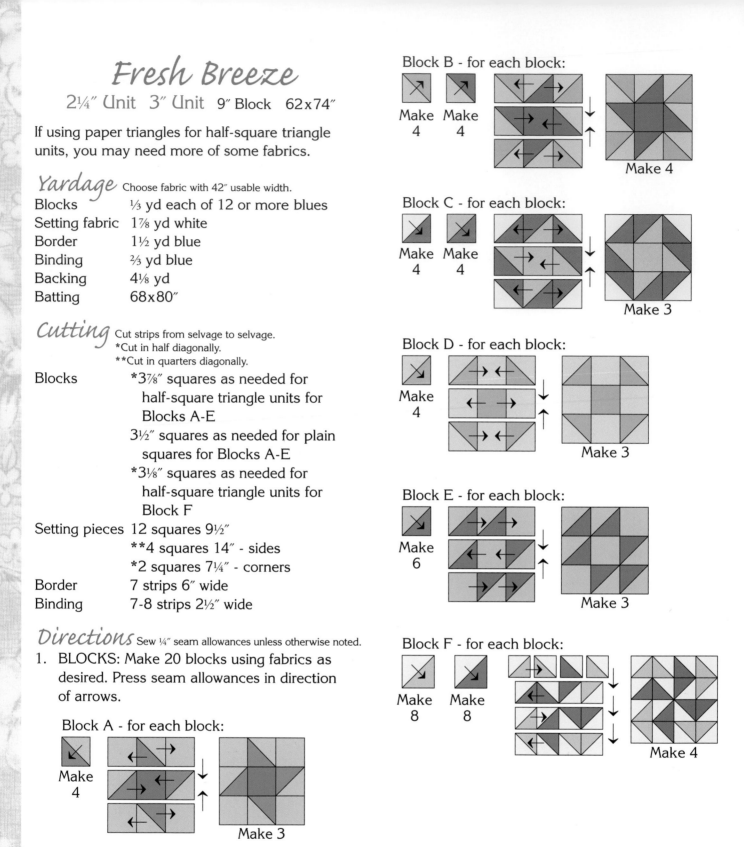

Block A - for each block:
Make 4
Make 3

Block B - for each block:
Make 4 Make 4
Make 4

Block C - for each block:
Make 4 Make 4
Make 3

Block D - for each block:
Make 4
Make 3

Block E - for each block:
Make 6
Make 3

Block F - for each block:
Make 8 Make 8
Make 4

Continued on page 39

FRESH *Breeze*

Happy Days

15″ Block   57x72″

Yardage Choose fabric with 42″ usable width.

Blocks, Border 2	pastels graded from light to dark: 4 pinks, 4 greens, 4 oranges, 3 blues, 3 purples, 3 yellows
	⅝ yd each - darkest blue, purple, yellow
	⅜ yd each - all remaining fabrics
Border 1	¾ yd purple
Border 3	⅝ yd green
Binding	⅝ yd green
Backing	3¾ yd
Batting	63x78″

Cutting Cut strips from selvage to selvage.

Pastels
Assign letters A-C & A-D to each set of fabrics, from lightest to darkest.

Blocks	from each pink A, green A, orange A: 16 squares 3½″ - pinwheel bkgrnd
	from each pink B, green B, orange B: 2 strips 2″ wide - Log Cabin pieces
	from each pink C, green C, orange C: 3 strips 2″ wide - Log Cabin pieces
	from each pink D, green D, orange D: 3 strips 2″ wide - Log Cabin pieces
	from each blue A, purple A, yellow A: 2 strips 2″ wide - Log Cabin pieces
	from each blue B, purple B, yellow B: 3 strips 2″ wide - Log Cabin pieces
	from each blue C, purple C, yellow C: 16 squares 3½″ - folded triangles for pinwheels 4 strips 2″ wide - Log Cabin pieces 4 squares 2″ - folded triangles in block corners
Border 2	9-10 squares 2″ of each fabric
Border 1	6 strips 3½″ wide
Border 3	7 strips 2″ wide
Binding	7 strips 2½″ wide

Directions Sew ¼″ seam allowances unless otherwise noted.

1. BLOCKS: Make 4 pink and blue blocks, 4 purple and green blocks, and 4 yellow and orange blocks.

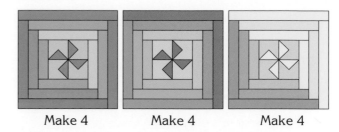

Make 4   Make 4   Make 4

For each block center, press squares for folded triangles as shown. Pin 2 folded triangles to right side of pinwheel background square as shown and place another background square right side down on top. Stitch right edge as shown. Open and press with seam allowance to left. Repeat. Stitch half-pinwheels together, opposing bulky seam allowances. Press. Repeat for remaining centers.

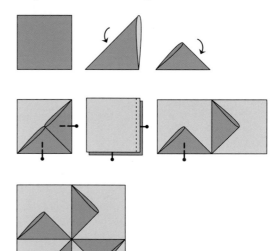

Continued on page 38

HAPPY *Days*

Oriental Garden

58x69"

Yardage Choose fabric with 42" usable width.

Center panel   1½ yd - if print is one-way directional, it must be on lengthwise grain

Border 1   ¼ yd
Border 2   ⅝ yd
Border 3   ¼ yd each of 10 fabrics
                6 for Strip Set 1 incl 2 accent fabrics
                4 for Strip Set 2
                ¼ yd - corner squares
Border 4   ⅝ yd
Binding   ⅝ yd
Backing   3⅞ yd
Batting   64x75"

Cutting Cut strips from selvage to selvage.

Center panel   36½x47½"
Border 1   5 strips 1¼" wide
Border 2   5 strips 3⅜" wide
Border 3   Strip Set 1 - accent fabrics
                3 strips of each fabric 1½" wide
                Strip Set 1 - remaining 4 fabrics
                3 strips of each fabric 2" wide
                Strip Set 2
                3 strips of each fabric 2½" wide
                Corner squares - 4 squares 6"
Border 4   7 strips 2½" wide
Binding   7 strips 2½" wide

Directions Sew ¼" seam allowances unless otherwise noted.

1. BORDER 1: Stitch strips together end to end using straight, not diagonal, seams. Press. Cut 2 pieces to fit sides of center panel. Stitch to center panel. Press seam allowances toward outside edge of quilt. Repeat at top and bottom.

2. BORDER 2: Repeat Step 1.

3. BORDER 3: Make 3 each of Strip Set 1 and Strip Set 2. Press. They must be 8½" wide from raw edge to raw edge. If not, adjust seam allowances and pressing. Crosscut strip sets into 8½" segments (9 from Set 1 & 11 from Set 2). To cut Border 3 triangles, place each segment right side up with the strips in the position shown. Make diagonal cuts as shown, all in the same direction for Set 1, and all in the opposite direction for Set 2. Make separate piles of triangles: 1A, 1B, 2A, and 2B.

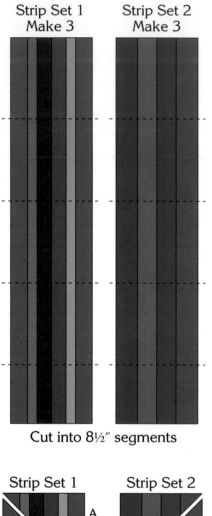

Strip Set 1 Make 3   Strip Set 2 Make 3

Cut into 8½" segments

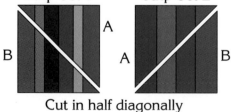

Strip Set 1   Strip Set 2

Cut in half diagonally

Continued on page 44

ORIENTAL *Garden*

Indigo & Eggplant

3″ Unit   6″ Unit   19½″ Block   70x91″

If using paper triangles for half-square triangle units, you may need more of some fabrics.

Yardage Choose fabric with 42″ usable width.

Blocks	purple/gold units	1¼ yd dark purple
		1¼ yd medium purple
		¾ yd gold
	teal units	1⅞ yd dark teal
		1⅓ yd turquoise
	center squares	⅛ yd orange
	center strips	1 yd black
Sashing		⅞ yd orange
Border		1¼ yd black
Binding		¾ yd black
Backing		5¾ yd
Batting		76x97″

Cutting Cut strips from selvage to selvage.
*Cut in half diagonally.

Blocks	purple/gold units	*24 squares 6⅞″ - dark purple
		*24 squares 6⅞″ - med purple
		48 squares 4″ - gold
	teal units	48 squares 3½″ - dark teal
		*96 squares 3⅞″ - dark teal
		*96 squares 3⅞″ - turquoise
	center squares	12 squares 2″
	center strips	48 pieces 2x9½″
Sashing		16 strips 1½″ wide
Border		8 strips 4½″ wide
Binding		9 strips 2½″ wide

Directions Sew ¼″ seam allowances unless otherwise noted.

1. BLOCKS: Make 12 blocks as shown. Press seam allowances to dark teal in small units and to purple in large units. See arrows on diagram. Press seam allowances toward black center strips when quarter-blocks are sewn together.

For each block:

Make 16   Make 4   Make 4

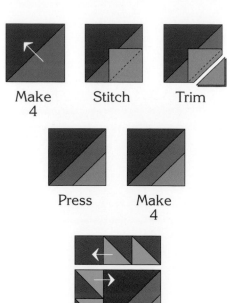

Make 4   Stitch   Trim

Press   Make 4

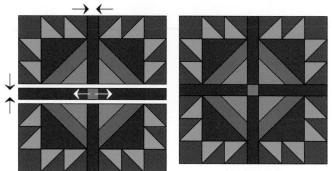

Make 4 quarter-blocks

Make 12

2. ASSEMBLE: Cut 8 pieces 20″ long from sashing strips. Stitch blocks in rows with sashing strips between them. See diagram. Press seam allowances toward sashing. Stitch remaining sashing strips end to end. Press. Cut 3 to same width as rows. Stitch rows of blocks and sashing together. Press seam allowances toward sashing. Cut 2 pieces to fit sides of quilt. Stitch to sides of quilt. Press seam allowances toward sashing. Repeat at top and bottom. Diagram on page 36.

Continued on page 36

INDIGO & *Eggplant*

Make Mine Hot
4″ Unit   16″ Block   67x67″

If using paper triangles for half-square triangle units, you may need more of some fabrics.

Yardage Choose fabric with 42″ usable width.

Blocks	corner squares	½ yd each of 5 teals
	side units	⅜ yd each of 4 teals
	star points	⅜ yd dark red-orange
		¼ yd medium red-orange
		⅜ yd light red-orange
	4-patches	⅙ yd each - 2 reds, 2 oranges, 1 yellow, 2 purples
	center triangles	¼ yd each - dark blue-purple, medium purple, yellow-orange (ours are variegated fabrics)
Sashing	squares	⅛ yd teal
	rectangles	1 yd orange
Border 1		⅝ yd light purple
Border 2		1 yd purple
Binding		⅔ yd purple
Backing		4⅜ yd
Batting		73x73″

Cutting Cut strips from selvage to selvage.
*Cut in half diagonally.

Blocks	corner squares	6 strips 2½″ wide - each fabric
	side units	*36 squares 4⅞″ - teals
	star points	*16 squares 4⅞″ - dk red-orange
		*4 squares 4⅞″ - med red-orange
		*16 squares 4⅞″ - lt red-orange
	4-patches	36 squares 3⅜″ - 5-6 of each fabric
	center triangles	*8 squares 4⅞″ - dark blue-purple
		*8 squares 4⅞″ - medium purple
		*2 squares 4⅞″ - yellow-orange
Sashing	squares	16 squares 2½″
	rectangles	24 pieces 2½x16½″
Border 1		6 strips 2½″ wide
Border 2		7 strips 4¼″ wide
Binding		7-8 strips 2½″ wide

Directions Sew ¼″ seam allowances unless otherwise noted.

1. BLOCKS: Using pattern, diagrams, and directions on page 48, paper piece 36 corner squares with 2½″ teal strips. Use fabrics in different positions in different squares. Press.

Make 9 four-patch units using 3⅜″ squares, varying placement of fabrics in each. Press seam allowances in direction of arrows. To four-patch units, stitch triangles cut from dark blue-purple, medium purple, and yellow-orange 4⅞″ squares as shown. Press seam allowances toward outside of unit.

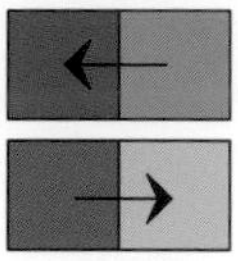

Make 9
Vary fabric placement

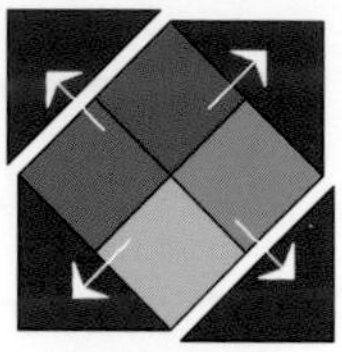

Make 4
4-patches will vary

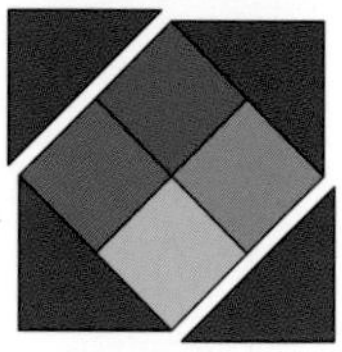

Make 4
4-patches will vary

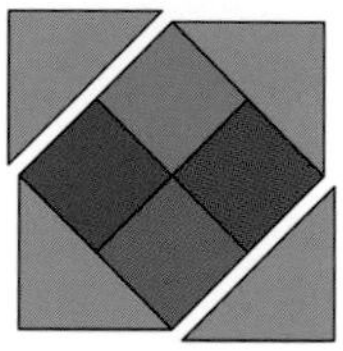

Make 1
4-patch will vary

Continued on page 37

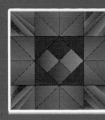

Park Avenue
2″ Border Unit   12″ Block   48x60″

If using paper triangles for half-square triangle units in Border 1, you may need more of some fabrics.

Yardage Choose fabric with 42″ usable width.

Blocks	background	1 yd light blue
	corners	½ yd each of teal, aqua
	star points	½ yd each of 2 browns
	center bkgrnd	½ yd aqua
	center stars	⅜ yd teal
Border 1		½ yd each light blue, brown
Border 2	sides	¾ yd teal
	corners	⅙ yd brown
Binding		⅝ yd teal
Backing		3¼ yd
Batting		54x66″

Cutting Cut strips from selvage to selvage.
*Cut in half diagonally.

Blocks	background	48 pieces 4x5½″
	corners	24 squares 4″ each fabric
	star points	48 squares 3″ each brown
	center bkgrnd	48 squares 2″
		48 pieces 2x2½″
	center stars	12 squares 2½″
		96 squares 1½″
Border 1	sides	*42 squares 2⅞″ - light blue
	corners	4 squares 2½″ - light blue
	sides	*42 squares 2⅞″ - brown
Border 2	sides	5 strips 4½″ wide - teal
	corners	4 squares 4½″ - brown
Binding		6 strips 2½″ wide

Directions Sew ¼″ seam allowances unless otherwise noted.

1. BLOCKS: Make 12 center stars with aqua and teal as shown. Press seam allowances in direction of arrows. Make 24 large star point units with each brown as shown. Stitch center stars, brown star point units and corners into blocks as shown. Press seam allowances in direction of arrows.

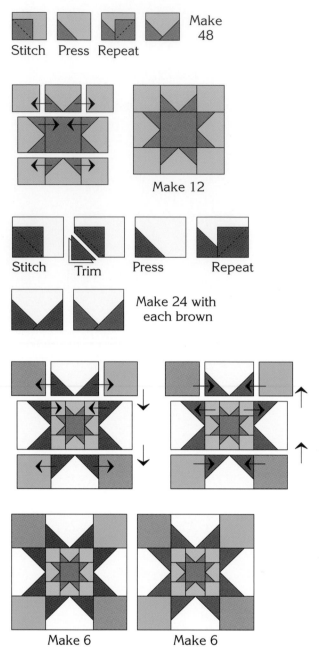

Make 48

Stitch Press Repeat

Make 12

Stitch Trim Press Repeat

Make 24 with each brown

Make 6   Make 6

2. ASSEMBLE: Arrange blocks in a setting of 3 across and 4 down, alternating large star point fabrics and making sure corner squares are oriented as shown. Diagram on page 42. Stitch blocks into horizontal rows. Press seam allowances to right in odd rows and to left in even rows. Stitch rows together. Press long horizontal seam allowances down or open.

Continued on page 42

Sunflower Fields

3" Unit 4¼" Unit 6" Unit 53 x 53"

If using paper triangles for half-square triangle units, you may need more of some fabrics.

To eliminate the applique in this quilt, choose an alternate coloration with more darks and/or mediums in the center panel.

Yardage Choose fabric with 42" usable width.

Center panel	½ yd each of 2 creams
	¼ yd each of 2 greens
Corner units	¼ yd each of 2 tans (1 light, 1 medium), 4 greens, 2 rusts, 1 brown
Applique	⅛ yd each of 3-4 greens - leaves
	⅙ yd green - stems
	¼ yd each of 2 golds - sunflowers
	⅛ yd each of 3 rusts & browns - sunflower centers
	⅛ yd rust - square applique
Border 1	¼ yd
Border 2	½ yd each brown, rust - triangle units
	⅙ yd rust - corner squares
Border 3	¼ yd green
Border 4	1 yd rust
Binding	⅝ yd rust
Backing	3½ yd
Batting	59 x 59"

Cutting Cut strips from selvage to selvage.
*Cut in half diagonally.

Center panel	*7 squares 6⅞" of each cream
	*1 square 6⅞" of each green
Corner units	*2 squares 5⅛" of light tan
	*6 squares 5⅛" of medium tan
	*4 squares 5⅛" of each of 3 greens
	8 pieces 3 x 4¾" of remaining green
	*2 squares 5⅛" of 1 rust
	8 pieces 2¼ x 4¾" of remaining rust
	*2 squares 5⅛" of brown
Applique	see pages 46-47
Border 1	4 strips 1½" wide
Border 2	*24 squares 3⅞" of each brown, rust
	4 squares 3½" - corners
Border 3	5 strips 1⅛" wide
Border 4	5 strips 5½" wide
Binding	6 strips 2½" wide

Directions Sew ¼" seam allowances unless otherwise noted.

1. CENTER PANEL: Make units as shown. Lightly finger press seam allowances so direction can be easily changed. Arrange units as shown. As you stitch units into horizontal rows, position all seam allowances in direction of arrows. Press. Stitch rows together. Press in direction of arrows.

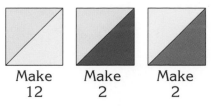

Make 12   Make 2   Make 2

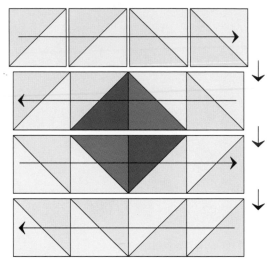

2. CORNER UNITS: Make units as shown, pressing seam allowances in direction of arrows.

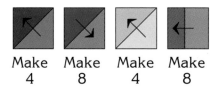

Make 4   Make 8   Make 4   Make 8

Adding green and medium tan triangles, arrange units as shown in diagram on page 41. Stitch into horizontal rows. Press seam allowances in direction of arrows. Stitch rows together. Press in direction of arrows. Make 4. Stitch corner units to center panel.

Continued on page 41

SUNFLOWER *Fields*

Flower Power

1½" Unit   3" Unit   9" Block   62x72"

If using paper triangles for half-square triangle units, you may need more of some fabrics.

Yardage Choose fabric with 42" usable width.

Blocks, sashing, Border 2
⅔ yd each - pink, blue, yellow, purple
⅜ yd each - orange, red, turquoise
Blocks, sashing, Borders 1 & 3
3¼ yd black
Blocks, Border 2
1 yd green (ours is a variegated fabric)
Binding   ⅝ yd black
Backing   4 yd
Batting   68x78"

Cutting Cut strips from selvage to selvage.
*Cut in half diagonally.

Brights	blocks	*24 squares 3⅞" each of pink & blue - pinwheels
		*12 squares 3⅞" each of yellow, orange, red, purple, turquoise - pinwheels
		*48 squares 2⅜" each of yellow, pink, purple, blue - points
	sashing	20 squares 1½"
	Border 2	*5-6 squares 3⅞" of each fabric
Black	blocks	120 squares 1⅝" - centers
		120 squares 2" - bkground corners
		*240 squares 2⅜" - background
	sashing	49 pieces 1½x9½"
	Border 1	6 strips 2" wide
	Border 3	7 strips 2½" wide
Green	blocks	*12 squares 3⅞" - pinwheels
		*48 squares 2⅜" - points
	Border 2	4 squares 3½" - corners
		*36 squares 3⅞"
		2 pieces 2½x3½" - side centers
		2 pieces 4½x3½" - top & bottom centers
Binding		7 strips 2½" wide

Directions Sew ¼" seam allowances unless otherwise noted.

1. BLOCKS: Make 6 each of the 5 blocks shown at right, pressing seam allowances in direction of arrows. To make each center pinwheel, press seam allowances of 2 units toward black

center and seam allowances of remaining 2 units toward colored triangles. Alternate these units when stitching the 4 together. Continue with construction of block.

For each block:

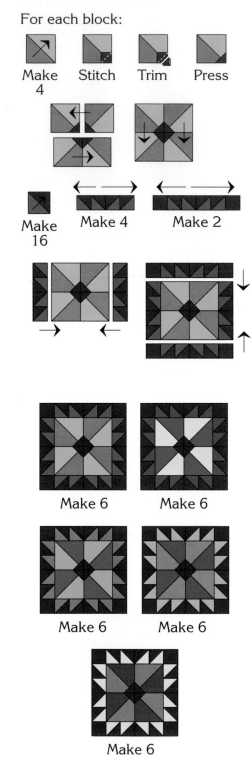

Make 4   Stitch   Trim   Press

Make 16   Make 4   Make 2

Make 6   Make 6

Make 6   Make 6

Make 6

Continued on page 40

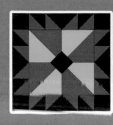

FLOWER *Power*

Just Triangles
Continued from page 16

Stitch units into rows. Press seam allowances in odd rows to right and in even rows to left. Stitch rows together. Press seam allowances down or open.

3. BORDERS: For each border, cut 2 pieces to fit sides of quilt. Stitch to quilt. Press seam allowances toward outside edge of quilt. Repeat at top and bottom.

4. LAYER & QUILT: Cut backing to same size as batting. Layer and quilt as desired. Trim backing and batting even with quilt top.

5. BIND: Stitch binding strips end to end. Press in half lengthwise, wrong sides together. Bind quilt using ⅜″ seam allowance.

Indigo & Eggplant
Continued from page 26

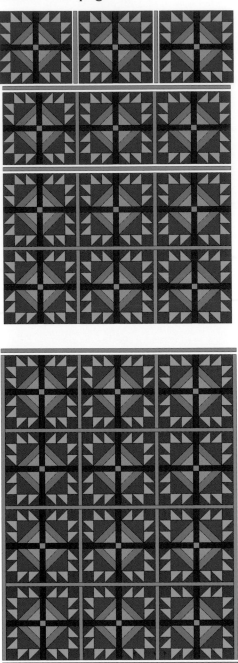

3. BORDER: Stitch strips together end to end using straight, not diagonal, seams. Press. Cut 2 pieces to fit sides of quilt. Stitch to quilt. Press seam allowances toward outside edge of quilt. Repeat at top and bottom.

4. LAYER & QUILT: Piece backing vertically to same size as batting. Layer and quilt as desired. Trim backing and batting even with quilt top.

5. BIND: Stitch binding strips end to end. Press in half lengthwise, wrong sides together. Bind quilt using ⅜″ seam allowance.

Make Mine Hot
Continued from page 28

Make 72 half-square triangle units with teal and red-orange triangles cut from 4⅛" squares, pairing as follows: 32 teal with dark red-orange, 32 teal with light red-orange, and 8 teal with medium red-orange. Use teals randomly or pair them for each block. Press seam allowances toward background fabric.

Stitch units into 9 blocks as shown. Press seam allowances in direction of arrows.

Make 8
for each block

Make 4
for each block

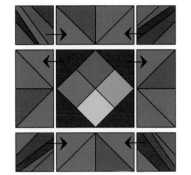

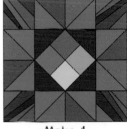

Make 4
Center 4-patches will vary

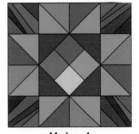

Make 4
Center 4-patches will vary

Make 1
Center 4-patch will vary

2. ASSEMBLE: Place blocks as shown, 4 with darkest star points in corners, 4 with lightest star points on sides, and remaining block in center. Stitch together rows of sashing rectangles and blocks. Stitch together rows of sashing squares and rectangles. Press seam allowances toward sashing. Stitch rows of sashing and rows of blocks together. Press seam allowances toward sashing.

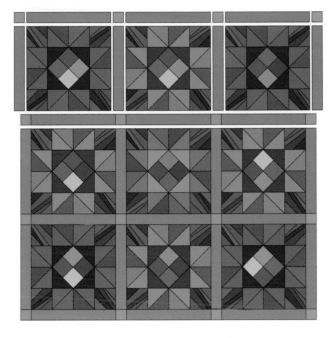

3. BORDERS: For each border, stitch strips together end to end using straight, not diagonal, seams. Press. Cut 2 pieces to fit sides of quilt. Stitch to quilt. Press seam allowances toward outside edge of quilt. Repeat at top and bottom.

4. LAYER & QUILT: Piece backing to same size as batting. Layer and quilt as desired. Trim backing and batting even with quilt top.

5. BIND: Stitch binding strips end to end. Press in half lengthwise, wrong sides together. Bind quilt using ⅜" seam allowance.

See chart below for cutting 2″ strips into pieces needed. Stitch Log Cabin pieces to pinwheel center in order shown for each round. Press with seam allowances toward outside of block. Repeat for remaining blocks.

LOG CABIN PIECES FOR BLOCKS - cut 4 pieces each size

	Piece #	Size	Pink/Blue Blocks Fabric	Green/Purple Blocks Fabric	Orange/Yellow Blocks Fabric
Round 1	#1	6½″	pink B	green B	orange B
	#2	8″	pink B	green B	orange B
	#3	8″	blue A	purple A	yellow A
	#4	9½″	blue A	purple A	yellow A
Round 2	#1	9½″	pink C	green C	orange C
	#2	11″	pink C	green C	orange C
	#3	11″	blue B	purple B	yellow B
	#4	12½″	blue B	purple B	yellow B
Round 3	#1	12½″	pink D	green D	orange D
	#2	14″	pink D	green D	orange D
	#3	14″	blue C	purple C	yellow C
	#4	15½″	blue C	purple C	yellow C

Round 1   Round 2 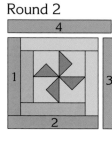 Round 3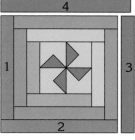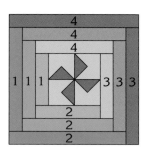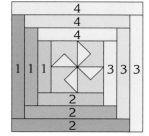

Numbers indicate piece # and order of stitching for each round

2. ASSEMBLE: For folded triangles in block corners, press 2″ squares in half diagonally, wrong side inside. Arrange blocks as shown. Pick up blocks one at a time and pin folded triangles to corners as shown, matching raw edges of folded triangle to raw edges of quilt block. Stitch blocks into rows. Press. Stitch rows together. Press.

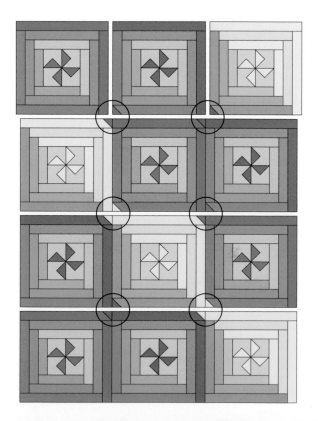

3. BORDER 1: Stitch strips end to end using straight, not diagonal, seams. Press. Cut 2 pieces to fit sides of quilt. Stitch to quilt. Press seam allowances toward outside edge of quilt. Repeat at top and bottom.

4. BORDER 2. Press thirty-eight 2″ squares in half diagonally, wrong side inside. Pin one to each of 38 other squares, mixing colors as desired. For side borders, stitch squares together with folded-triangle units scattered randomly. Press. If necessary, adjust a few seams to make borders fit quilt. Stitch side borders to quilt. Press seam allowances toward Border 1. Repeat for top and bottom borders.

Sides - 44 units - Make 2

Top & Bottom- 36 units - Make 2

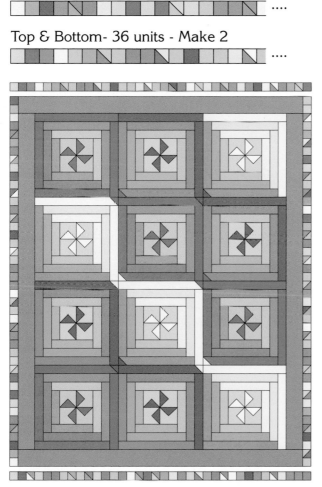

5. BORDER 3: Repeat Step 3.

6. LAYER & QUILT: Piece backing horizontally to same size as batting. Layer and quilt as desired. Trim backing and batting even with quilt top.

7. BIND: Stitch binding strips end to end. Press in half lengthwise, wrong sides together. Bind quilt using ⅜″ seam allowance.

Fresh Breeze
Continued from page 20

2. ASSEMBLE: Arrange blocks, setting squares, and setting triangles in a diagonal set as shown. Stitch blocks into diagonal rows. Press seam allowances toward setting squares and triangles. Stitch rows together. Press long seam allowances all one direction or open.

3. BORDER: Stitch strips together end to end using straight, not diagonal, seams. Press. Cut 2 pieces to fit sides of quilt. Stitch to quilt. Press seam allowances toward outside edge of quilt. Repeat at top and bottom.

4. LAYER & QUILT: Piece backing horizontally to same size as batting. Layer and quilt as desired. Trim backing and batting even with quilt top.

5. BIND: Stitch binding strips end to end. Press in half lengthwise, wrong sides together. Bind quilt using ⅜″ seam allowance.

Flower Power
Continued from page 34

2. ASSEMBLE: Stitch blocks and sashing rectangles together into rows. Press seam allowances toward sashing. Stitch sashing squares and sashing rectangles together into rows. Press seam allowances toward sashing rectangles. Stitch rows together. Press seam allowances toward sashing.

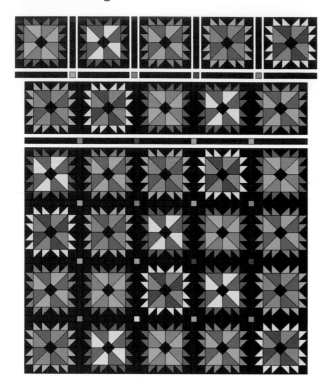

3. BORDER 1: Stitch strips end to end using straight, not diagonal, seams. Press. Cut 2 pieces to fit sides of quilt. Stitch to quilt. Press seam allowances toward outside edge of quilt. Repeat at top and bottom.

4. BORDER 2: Make 72 half-square triangle units, each with green on one side and one of the brights on the other. Press seam allowances toward green. For sides, stitch units together as shown with 2½x3½" green pieces at centers.

 Make 72

Sides - 20 units + center piece - Make 2

Top & Bottom
16 units + center piece + corner squares - Make 2

Press seam allowances toward center pieces. If necessary, adjust a few seams to make borders fit quilt. Stitch side borders to quilt. Press seam allowances toward Border 1. Repeat for top and bottom borders using 4½x3½" pieces at centers and adding 3½" squares at each end.

5. BORDER 3: Repeat Step 3.

6. LAYER & QUILT: Piece backing horizontally to same size as batting. Layer and quilt as desired. Trim backing and batting even with quilt top.

7. BIND: Stitch binding strips end to end. Press in half lengthwise, wrong sides together. Bind quilt using ⅜" seam allowance.

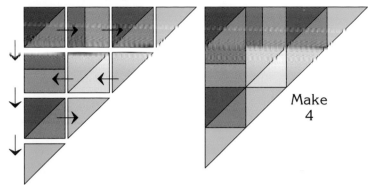

Make 4

3. APPLIQUE: Using diagram and photo as guides, place sunflowers on corners of center panel, then arrange leaves and stems. Trim stem lengths as needed and hide ends under sunflowers and other stems. When arrangement is pleasing, fuse all applique pieces. Fuse square applique to center of panel. Stitch edges of appliques using machine blanket stitch or zigzag.

4. BORDER 1: Cut 2 pieces to fit sides of quilt. Stitch to quilt. Press seam allowances toward outside of quilt. Repeat at top and bottom.

5. BORDER 2: Make 48 half-square triangle units. Make 24 double units as shown, pressing seam allowances in direction of arrows. Stitch 12 units together for each side border. Press seam allowances in same direction as in double units. If necessary, adjust a few seams to make borders fit quilt. Stitch to sides of quilt. Press seam allowances toward Border 1. Repeat for top and bottom borders, adding squares to each end and pressing in direction of arrows.

6. BORDER 3: Stitch strips together end to end using straight, not diagonal, seams. Press. Cut 2 pieces to fit sides of quilt. Stitch to quilt. Press seam allowances toward outside edge of quilt. Repeat at top and bottom.

7. BORDER 4: Repeat Step 6.

8. LAYER & QUILT: Piece backing to same size as batting. Layer and quilt as desired. Trim backing and batting even with quilt top.

9. BIND: Stitch binding strips end to end. Press in half lengthwise, wrong sides together. Bind quilt using 3/8″ seam allowance.

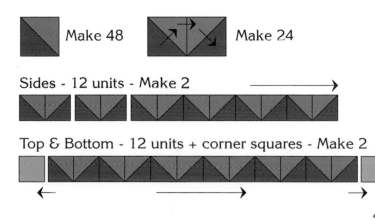

Make 48   Make 24

Sides - 12 units - Make 2

Top & Bottom - 12 units + corner squares - Make 2

Park Avenue
Continued from page 30

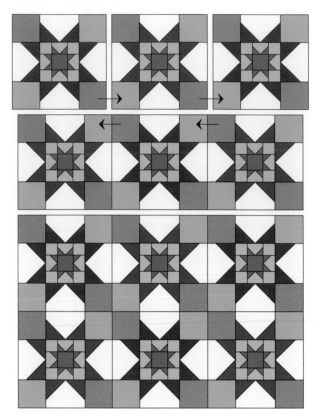

3. BORDER 1: Make 84 half-square triangle units. Lightly finger press seam allowances so direction can be easily changed. Stitch into pairs, opposing seam allowances as shown by arrows. For each side, stitch 12 pairs together as shown. Press seam allowances to right. If necessary, adjust a few seams to make borders fit quilt. Stitch to sides of quilt. Press seam allowances toward center of quilt. Repeat for each top and bottom border with 9 pairs, adding squares to each end.

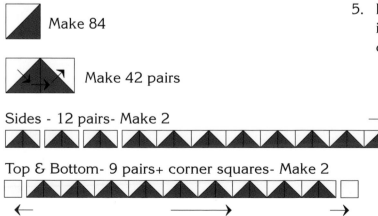

Make 84

Make 42 pairs

Sides - 12 pairs- Make 2

Top & Bottom- 9 pairs+ corner squares- Make 2

4. BORDER 2: Stitch strips end to end using straight, not diagonal, seams. Press. Cut 2 pieces to fit sides of quilt and 2 pieces to fit top and bottom of quilt. Stitch side borders to quilt. Press seam allowances toward outside edge of quilt. Stitch corner squares to ends of top and bottom borders. Stitch to quilt. Press seam allowances toward outside edge of quilt.

5. LAYER & QUILT: Piece backing horizontally to same size as batting. Layer and quilt as desired. Trim backing and batting even with quilt top.

6. BIND: Stitch binding strips end to end. Press in half lengthwise, wrong sides together. Bind quilt using ⅜″ seam allowance.

Domino Effect
Continued from page 8

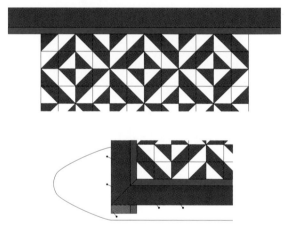

4. LAYER & QUILT: Piece backing vertically to same size as batting. Layer and quilt as desired. Trim backing and batting even with quilt top.

5. BIND: Stitch binding strips end to end. Press in half lengthwise, wrong sides together. Bind quilt using ⅜″ seam allowance.

Continued from page 18

Make Row Sets 2, 4, and 6 the same way, except for direction of pressing seam allowances. See diagram.

Row Sets 2, 4, 6

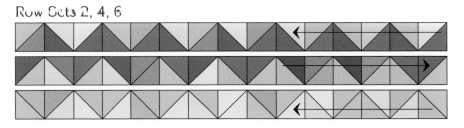

Make Row Set 7, pressing seam allowances as shown.

Row Set 7

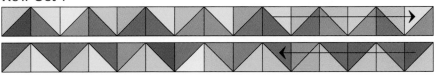

2. ASSEMBLE: Stitch Row Sets together. Press long horizontal seam allowances down or open.

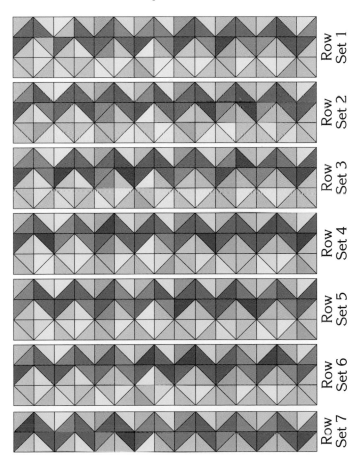

Row Set 1
Row Set 2
Row Set 3
Row Set 4
Row Set 5
Row Set 6
Row Set 7

3. BORDERS: For each border, stitch strips together end to end using straight, not diagonal, seams. Press. Cut 2 pieces to fit sides of quilt. Stitch to quilt. Press seam allowances toward outside edge of quilt. Repeat at top and bottom.

4. LAYER & QUILT: Piece backing horizontally to same size as batting. Layer and quilt as desired. Trim backing and batting even with quilt top.

5. BIND: Stitch binding strips end to end. Press in half lengthwise, wrong sides together. Bind quilt using ⅜" seam allowance.

Oriental Garden
Continued from page 24

Stitch triangles together as shown, alternating 2A and 2B along outside edge
and 1A and 1B along inside edge. Press. Trim ends of each border as shown,
wrong side up, ¼″ from a line perpendicular to bottom edge of triangle and
running through top point of triangle.

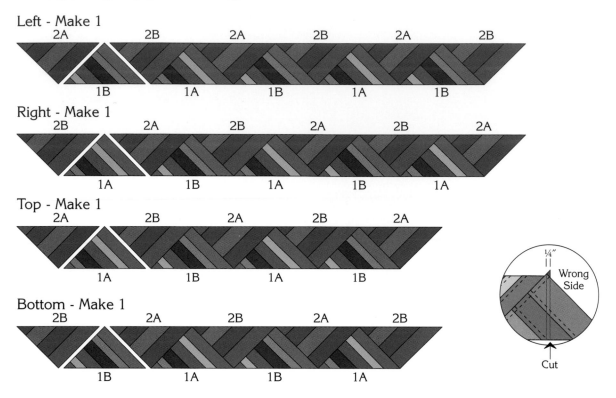

Left - Make 1

Right - Make 1

Top - Make 1

Bottom - Make 1

With Border 3 next to sewing machine feed dog to
control bias edges, stitch each side border to quilt.
Press seam allowances toward Border 2. Stitch
corner squares to ends of top and bottom borders.
Stitch borders to quilt. Press seam allowances
toward Border 2.

4. BORDER 4: Repeat Step 1 on page 24 with
   Border 3 next to feed dog.

5. LAYER & QUILT: Piece backing horizontally to
   same size as batting. Layer and quilt as desired.
   Trim backing and batting even with quilt top.

6. BIND: Stitch binding strips end to end. Press in
   half lengthwise, wrong sides together. Bind quilt
   using ⅜″ seam allowance.

MORE COLORATIONS & LAYOUTS *for Triangle Units*

Quilts of many different sizes can be made from these diagrams by varying the size of the half-square triangle unit and planning borders based on the desired quilt size.

88 Units - 1 cream, 5 greens, 1 pink

192 Units - 1 black, 12 jewel tones

192 Units - 1 white, pastels in 7 colors

432 Units - 10 yellows, 10 jewel tones

Sunflower Fields

Trace 4 of each

Use this layout as a guide for placement

Applique patterns are for fusible web, reversed for tracing & no seam allowances added

Trace 1

Trace 4 of each

46

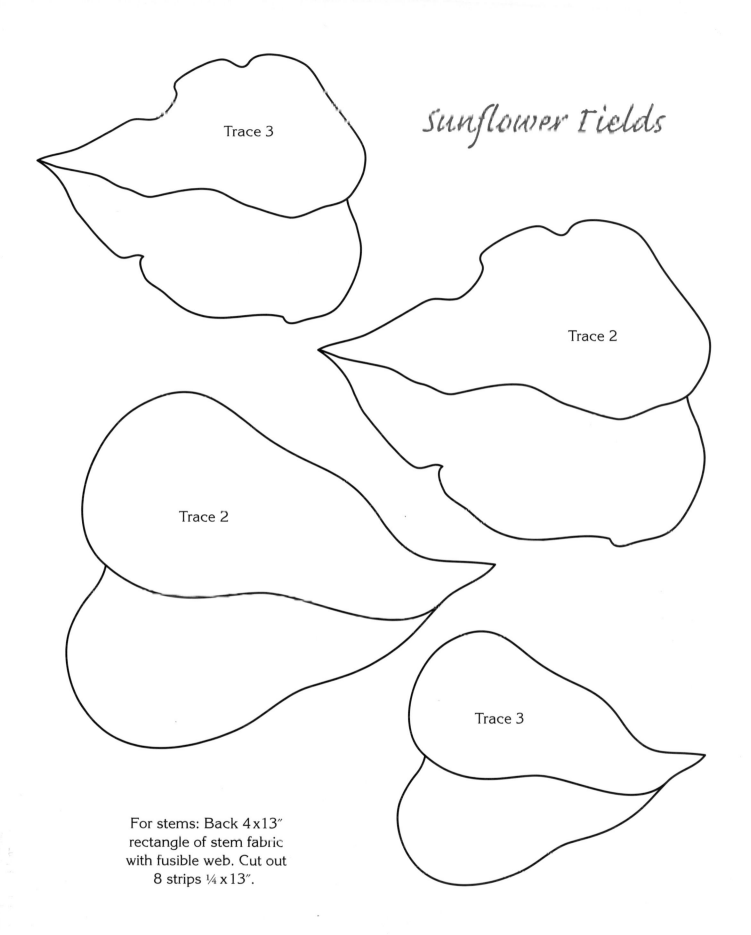

Trace 3

sunflower fields

Trace 2

Trace 2

Trace 3

For stems: Back 4 x 13″ rectangle of stem fabric with fusible web. Cut out 8 strips ¼ x 13″.

Make Mine Hot

Make 18 copies of this page
for paper piecing corner squares.
Cut each square out leaving ¼"
margin beyond dotted line.

Permission granted to copy for personal use.

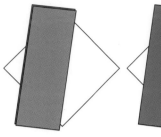

Place 2 strips right sides together. Place on wrong side of pattern, overlapping one of center diagonal lines by ¼". Flip pattern over and stitch on line.

Press top piece to right side.

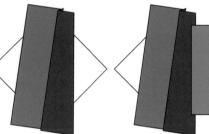

Fold paper on next diagonal line and trim second strip ¼" from diagonal line.

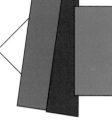

Add a third strip of fabric in same way. Rotate square and add fourth and fifth strips to other side in same way. Trim square on dotted line. Remove paper now or wait until after block is sewn.

Make 36

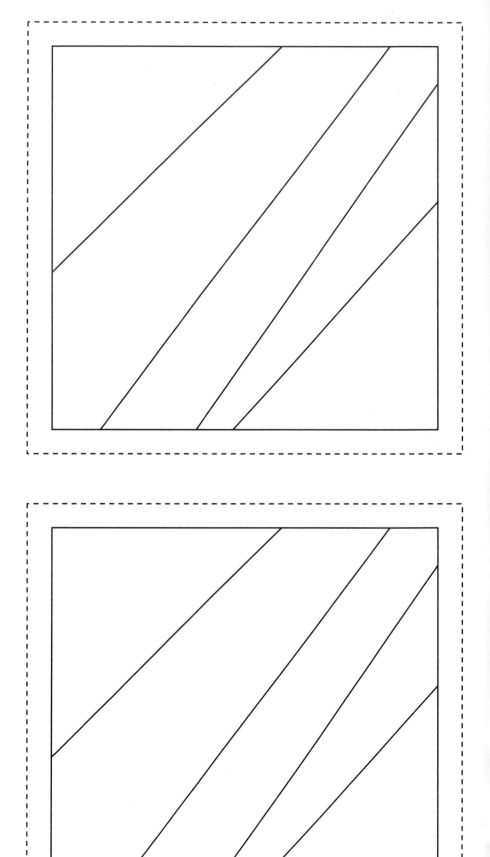